CHRISTMAS HOME MA

Festive Projects and 10 Easy Patterns
for Holiday Decorating

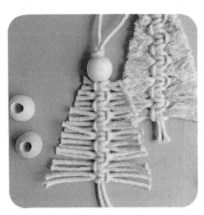

TABLE OF CONTENTS

1. **INTRODUCTION**................... 01

Tools that you need 02

2. **TYPES OF STITCHES**

Chain Stitch 06

Single Stitch 07

Slip Stitch 08

Half Double Stitch 08

Double Stitch 09

Increase Stitch 10

Invisible Decrease Stitch...........10

Fastening Off 11

3. **ABBREVIATIONS** 12

4. **MACRAME PATTERNS**

Striped Ball 14

Diamond Ball 20

Braided Macrame 25

Christmas Macrame 30

Gnomes Macrame. 39

Wreath Macrame 49

Rustic Ornament Macrame 54

Ring Ornament Macrame 58

Tree Ornament Macrame 63

Christmas Ornament Macrame 67

5. **THANK YOU**......................70

INTRODUCTION

Welcome to *Christmas Home Macramé: Festive Projects and 10 Easy Patterns for Holiday Decorating*

This book is your gateway to a world of creativity and holiday spirit, where the timeless art of macramé meets the warmth of the Christmas season. Here, you'll discover various enchanting projects designed to elevate your holiday décor—from whimsical ornaments and elegant garlands to stunning wall hangings and thoughtful gifts. Whether you're a seasoned macramé enthusiast or just starting your crafting journey, each project features clear instructions and helpful tips, making it easy to create beautiful pieces that add a personal touch to your celebrations. As you knot and weave, you'll find joy in the process, transforming simple materials into heartfelt treasures.

Let *Christmas Home Macramé: Festive Projects and 10 Easy Patterns for Holiday Decorating* inspire you to gather friends and family, celebrate creativity, and fill your home with the magic of handmade holiday charm. Let's get started and make this Christmas truly special!

A CROCHET HOOK

CROCHET HOOKS STYLES

- Inline (or Straight) Crochet Hooks: These types of hooks have a deeper throat and are pointier tips with a flatter thumb rest that, according to some, can help with tension and gauge in patterns.

- Inline (or Straight) Crochet Hooks: These types of hooks have a deeper throat and are pointier tips with a flatter thumb rest that, according to some, can help with tension and gauge in patterns.

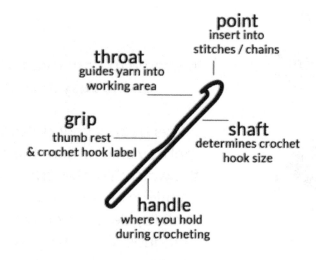

point
insert into stitches / chains

throat
guides yarn into working area

grip
thumb rest & crochet hook label

shaft
determines crochet hook size

handle
where you hold during crocheting

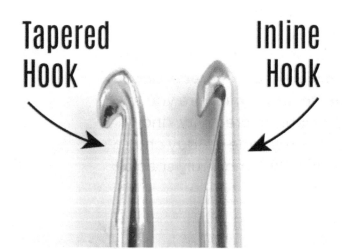

Tapered Hook

Inline Hook

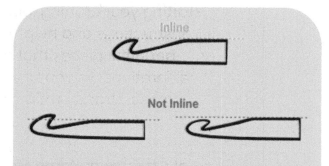

Inline

Not Inline

Inline hooks have the point in line with the shaft, while tapered hooks will have their point not in line with the shaft. On a tapered hook, the point can be either above or below the shaft's "line".

Common Hook Sizes

Hook	Names	Suggested Yarn Weights
	D/3.25mm	Super Fine and Fine(sock, sport, baby, fingering, 4-ply)
	E/3.50mm	Super Fine, Fine, and Light(sock, sport, baby, fingering, 4-ply, DK, light worsted, 8-ply)
	F/3.75mm	Fine and Light (sport, baby 4-ply, DK, light worsted, 8-ply)
	G/4.00mm	Light and Medium(DK, light worsted, 8-ply, worsted/heavy worsted, aran, 10-ply)
	H/5.00mm	Light and Medium(DK, light worsted, 8-ply, worsted/heavy worsted, aran, 10-ply)
	I/5.50mm	Medium and Bulky (worsted/heavy worsted, aran, 10-ply, chunky)
	J/6.00mm	Medium and Bulky (worsted/heavy worsted, aran, 10-ply, chunky)
	K/6.50mm	Bulky (chunky)
	N/9.00mm	Super Bulky (Super Chunky, Roving)

CROCHET HOOKS STYLES

The diameter of a hook shaft determines the size of the hook and the size of the stitches that are made. Hook sizes are measured in millimeters and are available from as small as 2 mm to 20 mm or larger!

YARN

FIBER YARN BASIC

Yarn is a continuous strand of intertwined fibers that are held together by their mutual friction. While this is quite a mouthful, all it means is that the individual fiber strands are twisted together so that their rough outer surfaces adhere to one another.

Animal fibers – wool, alpaca, cashmere, etc.
- Benefits: warm, elastic, breathable.
- Disadvantages: can be irritating to the skin, cost prohibitive, special care instructions, tough to find in big box stores.

Plant fibers – cotton, bamboo, linen, etc.
- Benefits: moisture-wicking, breathable, sustainable. Disadvantages: heavier fibers, inelastic, color can fade.

Synthetic fibers – acrylic, nylon, polyester, etc.
- Benefits: affordable, accessible, easy care.
- Disadvantages: environmental impacts, pilling issues, wide variation in quality.

YARN WEIGHTS

CRAFT YARN COUNCIL
THE INDUSTRY STANDARD FOR YARN WEIGHTS

Super Fine	Fine	Light	Medium	Bulky	Super Bulky	Jumbo
Very lightweight, popular for socks and shawls	Lightweight yarn, popular for baby and indoor sweaters	Somewhat lightweight, popular for garments and accessories	Most popular weight, for almost any project	A bit heavier weight than worsted, popular for sweaters and afghans	Heavier weight yarn, popular for statement accessories	Heaviest weight, popular for bold accent pieces

YARN STORAGE AND FINISHED PROJECT CARE

Machine Wash Cold

Machine Wash Warm

Machine Wash Hot

Hand Wash

Do Not Wash

STITCHES

CHAIN (CH)

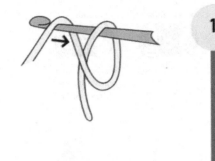

1 — Use the hook to draw the yarn through the loop

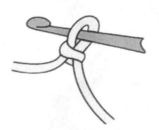

2 — Pull the loop until tight

3 — Wrap the yarn over the hook from back to front. Pull the hook, carrying the yarn, through the loop already on your hook.

4 — You have now completed one chain stitch. Repeat these steps as indicated in the pattern to create a foundation chain.

SINGLE CROCHET (SC)

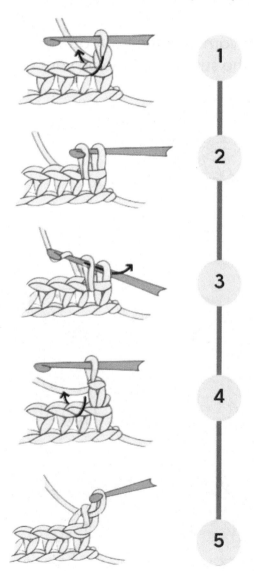

1 Insert the hook into the next stitch

2 Wrap the yarn over the hook. Pull the yarn through the stitch

3 You will see that there are now two loops on the hook. Wrap the yarn over the hook again and draw it through both loops at once

4 You have now completed one single crochet

5 Insert the hook into the next stitch to continue

SLIP STITCH (SLST)

Insert your hook into the next stitch

Wrap the yarn over the hook and draw through the stitch and loop on your hook at once

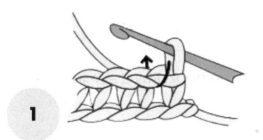

1

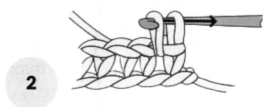

2

HALF DOUBLE CROCHET (HDC)

- Bring your yarn over the hook from back to front before placing the hook in the stitch

- Wrap the yarn over the hook and draw the yarn through the stitch. You now have three loops on the hook

- Wrap the yarn over the hook again and pull it through all three loops on the hook

- You have completed your first half double crochet. To continue, bring your yarn over the hook and insert it in the next stitch

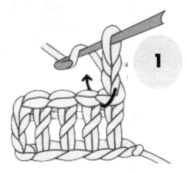

1

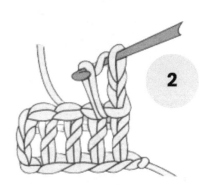

2

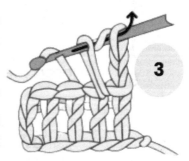

3

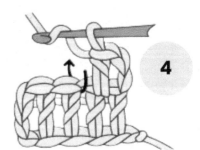

4

DOUBLE CROCHET (DC)

1 When starting a new row of double crochet, work three chain stitches to gain height. Bring your yarn over the hook from back to front before placing the hook in the stitch

2 Wrap the yarn over the hook and draw the yarn through the stitch. You now have three loops on the hook

3 Wrap the yarn over the hook again and pull it through the first two loops on the hook

4 You now have two loops on the hook. Wrap the yarn over the hook one last time and draw it through both loops on the hook

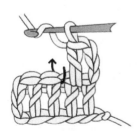

5 You have now completed one double crochet. To continue, bring your yarn over the hook and insert it in the next stitch

INCREASE (INC)

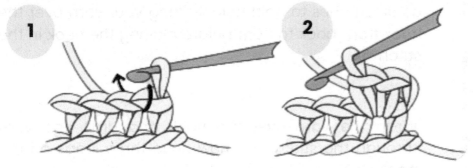

To increase you make two (single) crochet stitches in the next stitch.

INVISIBLE DECREASE ((INV) DEC)

- Insert the hook in the front loop of your first stitch. Now immediately insert your hook in the front loop of the second stitch

- You now have three loops on your hook. Wrap the yarn over the hook and draw it through the first two loops on your hook

- Wrap the yarn over again and draw it through the two loops remaining on your hook

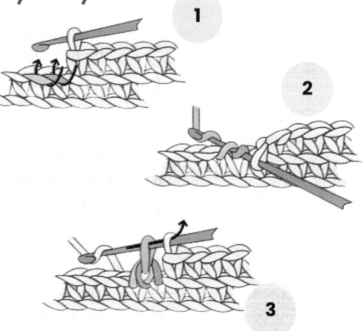

FASTENING OFF

When you've finished crocheting, cut the yarn a couple of inches 7 cm from your last stitch. Pull the yarn through the last loop until it is all the way through

- You now have a finished knot. Thread the long tail through a tapestry needle and insert your tapestry needle through the back loop of the next stitch
- This way the finishing knot will remain hidden in your finished piece. You can use this piece of yarn to continue sewing the pieces together.

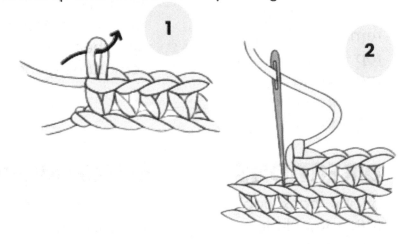

ABBREVIATION

GENERAL

alt - alternate
approx - approximately
beg - beginning
bet - between
cont - continue
ch sp - chain space
foll - following
lp - loop
prev- previous
rem - remaining
rep - repeat
rnd - round
ws - wrong side
rs - right side

STITCHES

ch - chain stitch
sl st - slip stitch
sc - single crochet
hdc - half double crochet
dc - double crochet
tc - treble/triple crochet
dtr - double treble crochet
sh - shell
tch - turning chain

DIRECTIONS

bl/blo - back loop
fl/flo - front loop
bp - back post
dec - decrease
inc - increase
pm - place marker
sk - skip
yo/yoh - yarn over/hook

STITCH MODIFIERS

* Add these words to the
basic stitches
Bp - back post
FP - front post
ch chain stitch
e - extended
cl - cluster
2 tog - crochet 2 stitches
together (decrease)
pc - popcorn stitch

12

MEASUREMENTS

in- inch
cm- centimeter
oz- ounce
yd- yard
m- meter
mm- millimeter
g- gram

TOOLS

cc- contrast color
mc- main color
m- marker

SPECIAL TUNISIAN CROCHET TERMS

Fw P – forward pass
RetP – return pass
tfs – Tunisian full stitch
tks – Tunisian knit stitch
tps – Tunisian purl stitch
trs – Tunisian reverse stitch
tss – Tunisian simple stitch
ttw – Tunisian twisted

US AND UK TERM DIFFERENCES

US: slip stitch (sl st)
US: single crochet (sc)
US: half dc (hdc)
US: double crochet (dc)
US: treble (tr)
USL double treble (dtr)

UK: slip stitch (ss)
UK: double crochet (dc)
UK: half treble (htr)
UK: trebel (tr)
UK: double treble (dtr)
UK: triple treble (trtr)

13

Striped Ball

Materials

- Macrame (I used 1mm)
- Scissors
- Glass | Plastic Ball Ornaments

Step 1: Cut Macrame

Cut 14 pieces of 24 inch macrame (this depends on how large your ball is and how many stripes you want, you can do more or less) and one 12 inch piece.

Step 2: Knot Macrame

Use one of the 24 inch pieces as your main strand. Fold one of your other 24in strands in half and attach using a Lark's Head knot to the the middle of the main strand and tighten.

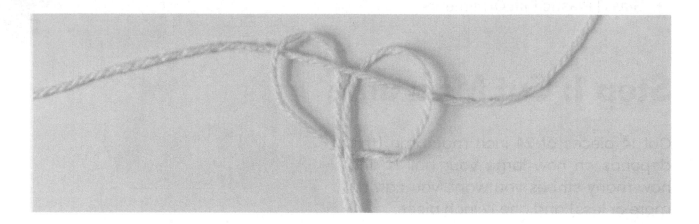

Step 3: Repeat Knots

Attach the other 24in pieces with the Lark's Head knot and center them on the main strand.

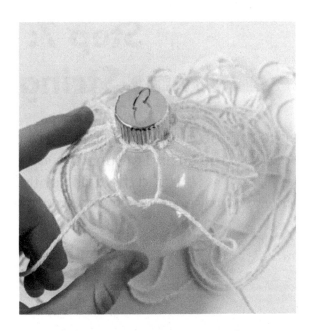

Step 4: Attach Strands

Loop the main strand around the top of the ball ornament. Tighten and knot it.

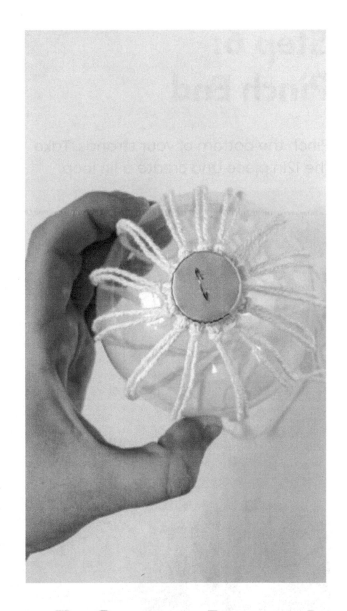

Step 5: Space Strands

Space all your strand pairs evenly out around the top.

Step 6: Pinch End

Pinch the bottom of your strands. Take the 12in piece and create a 1in loop.

Step 7: Wrap String

Leave the top of the string poking out and wrap the strand around the loop and the tails tightly.

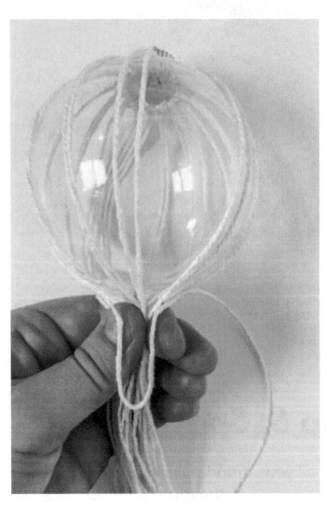

Step 8: End Loop

Continue wrapping your macrame till you get to the end of the strand. Stick the end through the loop we made at the beginning.

Step 9: Tighten

Pull the end of the strand that you left sticking out at the beginning. This will scoop your other end and the loop under your wrapped yarn.

Step 10: Trim

Trim any pieces sticking out of your loop and the tails to your desired length.

Diamond Ball

Materials

- Macrame (I used 1mm)
- Scissors
- Glass | Plastic Ball Ornaments

Step 1: Cut Macrame

Cut 14 pieces of 24 inch macrame (this depends on how large your ball is and how many stripes you want, you can do more or less) and one 12 inch piece.

Step 2: Knot Macrame

Use one of the 30in pieces as your main strand. Fold one of your other 30in strands in half and attach using a Lark's Head knot to the the middle of the main strand and tighten.

Step 3: Repeat Knots

Attach the other 30in pieces with the Lark's Head knot and center them on the main strand.

Step 4: Attach Strand

Loop the main strand around the top of the ball ornament. Tighten and knot it. Space all your knots out evenly around the top.

Step 5: Square Knot

Take two bordering strands (ie one strand from two different lark's head knots that are next to eachother). Cross the left over the right. It is important to remember which side crosses which as we will do the opposite side later.

Continue pulling the left strand down, around and over the right.

Now we switch to the opposite side. Cross the right over the left.

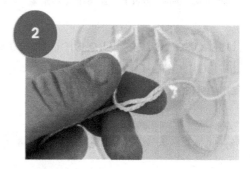

Continue pulling the right strand down, around and over the left. You now have a square knot. Tighten.

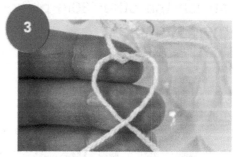

Step 6: Repeat Knots

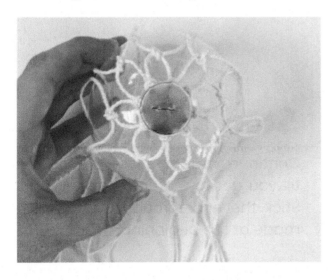 

Repeat the square knots on all the strands around the ornament.

Change directions with your strands and repeat the square knots. Continue this method till you get to the bottom.

Step 7: Pinch End

Pinch the bottom of your strands. Take the 12in piece and create a 1in loop.

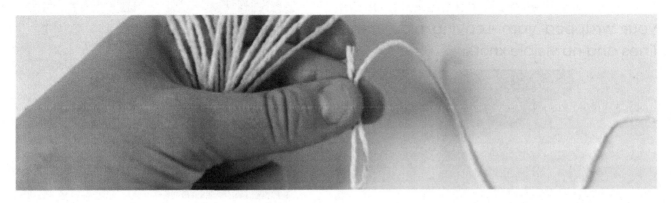

Step 8: Wrap String

Leave the top of the string poking out and wrap the strand around the loop and the tails tightly.

Step 9: End Loop

Continue wrapping your macrame till you get to the end of the strand. Stick the end through the loop we made at the beginning.

Step 10: Tighten

Pull the end of the strand that you left sticking out at the beginning. This will scoop your other end and the loop under your wrapped yarn. Leaving nice, clean lines and no visible knots.

Braided
Macrame

Materials

- Macrame (I used 1mm)
- Scissors
- Glass | Plastic Ball Ornaments

Step 1: Cut Macrame

Cut 10 pieces of 36 inch macrame (this depends on how large your ball is, you can do more or less) and one 12 inch piece.

Step 2: Knot Macrame

Use one of the 36in pieces as your main strand. Fold one of your other 36in strands in half and attach using a Lark's Head knot to the the middle of the main strand and tighten.

Step 3: Repeat Knots

Attach the other 30in pieces with the Lark's Head knot and center them on the main strand.

Step 4: Attach Strand

Loop the main strand around the top of the ball ornament. Tighten and knot it.

Step 5: Space Out Knots

Group your knots in pairs of two. Space the five sets evenly around the ball.

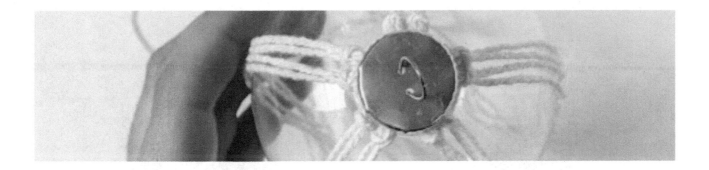

Step 6: Square Knots

We are going to focus on the two outer strands only. Take the right strand and cross it over the inner two and under the left.

Take the left strand and cross it under the inner strands and over the right. Pull tight and push to the top.

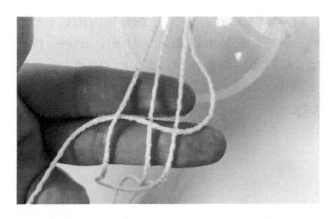
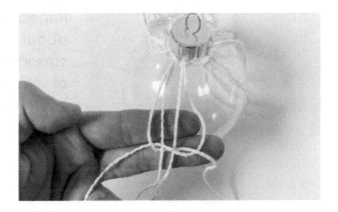

Repeat this but by starting with the opposite side first. If you use the same side again, your braid will start to spiral. Use the left side and cross it over the inner strands and under the right.

Take the right strand and cross it under the inner strands and over the left. Pull tight and push to the top.

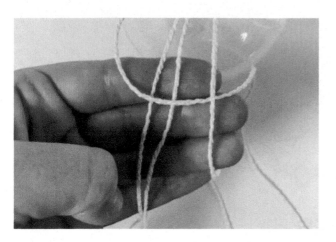

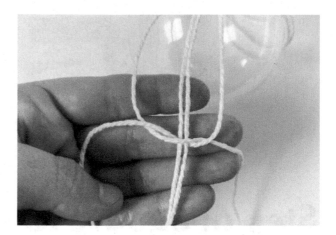

Step 7: Repeat Knot

Repeat the knots to your desired length, I did about 1.25in, on all five pairs. Then take two strands from two bordering pairs and do a couple of square knots about 1.25in away from the previous knots.

Step 8: Pinch End

Pinch the bottom of your strands. Take the 12in piece and create a 1in loop.

Step 9: Pinch End

Leave the top of the string poking out and wrap the strand around the loop and the tails tightly.

Step 10: End Loop

Continue wrapping your macrame till you get to the end of the strand. Stick the end through the loop we made at the beginning.

Step 11: Tighten

Pull the end of the strand that you left sticking out at the beginning. This will scoop your other end and the loop under your wrapped yarn. Leaving nice, clean lines and no visible knots.

Christmas Macrame

Materials

- Green macrame yarn (4mm)
- ivory macrame yarn
- Wool brush
- Comb
- Wooden ring or star
- Meaзuring tapе
- Scissors
- Wooden dowel rod
- Yarn needle
- Battery-operated fairy lights
- Fabric stiffener

The Body Of The Christmas Tree

I started out by folding two 160-inch pieces of macrame yarn in half and looping them onto the holes in the wooden star. Then I taped the star with duct tape to my kitchen counter.

The macrame Christmas tree pattern primarily uses diagonal Double Half Hitch knots (sometimes referred to as diagonal Clove Hitch knots, though they differ slightly in the yarn's crossing). Half Hitch Knots are loops attached to another piece of yarn or the dowel rod at the tree's base.

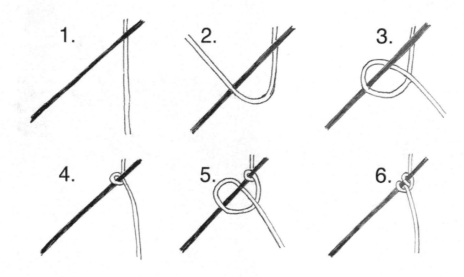

Make two Half Hitch knots right after the loops on the star.

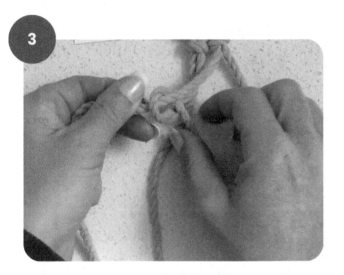

And then add one 160 inch piece of yarn folded in half onto the left and right side.

Add the strings using reversed Lark's Head knots, similar to the star but flipped to hide the loop. Next, add another row of diagonal Half Hitch knots, then attach more yarn pieces.

The below image is a guide to show where the extra yarn was added.

two pieces of yarn added with Lark's Head knots

one piece added on each side with reversed Lark's Head knot

one piece added on each side with reversed Lark's Head knot

one piece added on each side with reversed Lark's Head knot

two pieces added on each side with reversed Lark's Head knots

two pieces added on each side with reversed Lark's Head knots

two pieces added on each side with reversed Lark's Head knots

rows of diagonal Double Half Hitch knots to create a diamond pattern

I added an extra loop of Half Hitch knots on each side after the reversed Lark's Head knots to widen the tree without adding more yarn.

Next, I added a row of diagonal Half Hitch knots, then attached two 160" pieces on each side. Once I had 24 strings, I separated them into 3 groups of 8 to add the diamond pattern.

Time to make the diamond pattern.

The diamond center has 6 strings on the inside. I took that as a guide for the rest of them.

After that create diamonds all the way down. In the end, I had 4 diamonds at the bottom. Keep adding the rows of diamonds until you have the desired length of the tree.

Three times I added a second row of diagonal Half Hitch Knots to add some interest but that's also optional. Below you can see one of those double rows.

At the end, I added square knots to even out the rows before adding the dowel rod.

Attach the dowel rod to the macrame Christmas tree wallhanging by looping the 40 hanging strings into Half Hitch knots again around the rod. Since you cut 20 pieces of yarn at the beginning and then folded them in half to add them into the piece, you now ended up with 40 strings.

I combed the bottom fringe and soaked it in starch to prevent curling, then let it dry before trimming. I applied starch only to the bottom fringe and ivory tassel.

Adding The Tassels

Cut 8 pieces of ivory yarn at 16 inches long, fold them in half and loop them through the bottom center.

And it is exactly the same way that I added the green tassels afterward too. I opened and comb all the yarn but didn't add any starch.

Open and comb the yarn and after that trim the tassels. Mine are about 2.5 inches long.

Adding The Fairy Lights

Tied the battery pack of the fairy lights to the back of the tree as shown in my video. Then I threaded the lights through the tree using the wool needle. You don't really need the needle but I felt like it made it easier for sure.

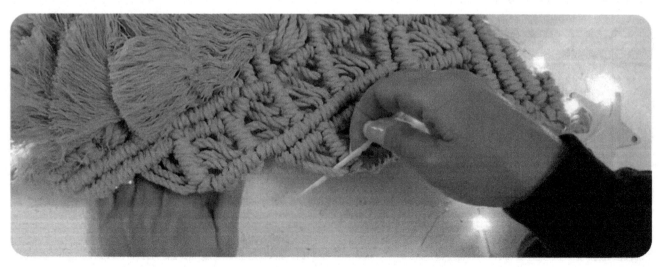

Gnomes
Macrame

Material

- 4mm ivory macrame cord
- Colored 3mm macrame yarn or 4mm macrame yarn (colored I used: green, blush, rust)
- Brown or natural wooden beads
- Scissors
- Hot glue and hot glue gun
- Wooden rings
- Comb
- Measuring tape
- Toilet paper rolls
- Clear packaging tape (optional)

Step 1: Cutting All The Macrame Yarn

- Beard measurements:

I only like using a 4 mm cord for the beard because it is nice and thick when unraveled. For the beard using 4 mm yarn, you need 8 strings that are around 9 inches long.

- Hat measurements:

For a hat made from 3 mm macrame yarn, you need 25 pieces (maybe you can squeeze an additional piece in there) of around 11 inches long.

For a hat that is made from 4 mm macrame yarn, you need 14 pieces of yarn that are 14 inches long.

- Mustache measurements:

You need 4 pieces of yarn that are 10 inches long for the mustache.

Making templates out of cardboard that can be used to wrap the yarn around. All you need to do is cut the ends of the wrapped yarn on one side and you have cut the yarn measurements in bulk.

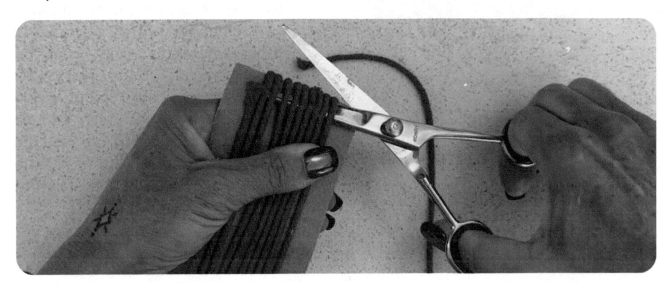

4mm macrame yarn for hat	3mm macrame yarn for hat	4mm macrame yarn for beard
2.5" x 7"	2.5" x 5.5"	2.5" x 4.5"

Here are the cardboard template measurements:

The macrame gnome kit idea involves using sandwich bags to package all the supplies needed to create a macrame gnome. Each kit contains pre-cut yarn and other materials and can be presented in gift bags or boxes for added charm. The creator made these kits as a special gift for their crafting-loving niece, aiming to enjoy some quality crafting time together during an upcoming visit to Germany.

Step 2: Make The Gnome's Beard

Loop all 8 pieces of macrame yarn that are 9-inch long onto the wooden ring by folding the cord in half and then using a lark's head knot as pictured below. After that use a comb to unravel all the macrame yarn for the beard of your gnome. Wait to trim the beard until the end.

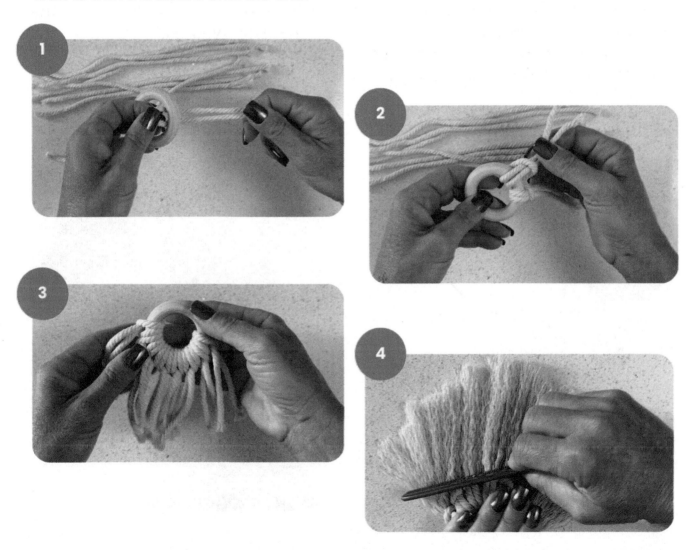

Step 3: Make The Mustache (Optional)

You can just use a wooden bead as the nose without adding yarn as a mustache. But I prefer to have a mustache. Plus that way you can't see the hole in the wooden bead.

Switch up the skin color of the gnome with different colored wooden beads.

Use the 4 strands that you cut earlier at 10 inches long and thread them through the hole of the wood bead. Then unravel and comb the yarn the same way you just did with the beard.

no mustache through wood bead nose

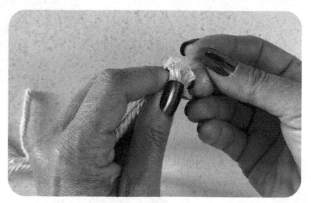

Step 4: Make The Hat

Cut a 0.75" piece from a toilet paper roll. Choose between a 3mm or 4mm yarn for the hat brim, and decide whether to use a regular or inverted Lark's Head Knot.

4mm macrame yarn with Lark's Head Knots

3mm macrame yarn with inverted Lark's Head Knots

3mm macrame yarn with Lark's Head Knots

The Lark's Head Knots are the same again as you did earlier for the beard.
Use a small piece of yarn to tie off the top of the hat and then trim the ends of the cords before unraveling, combing, and trimming them again.

If the toilet paper roll isn't that sturdy, you can wrap it with some clear packaging tape to make it more sturdy. The reason I'm mentioning this is that I've had the cardboard break twice already while making a gnome hat and then I had to start over again. Or just make sure you use a thicker sturdy toilet paper roll.

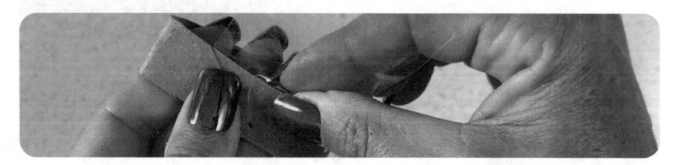

If you want to invert the Lark's Head Knots, you just have to add them to the toilet paper ring with the loop showing in the back instead of the front pictured above. And then all you have to do is stuff the string through the center of the toilet paper ring.

If you want to make macrame gnome ornaments and need them to hang for that purpose, then you can add a looped string as a hanger to the center of the hat.

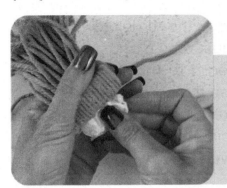

ANOTHER TIP: You can stuff the hat with cotton balls or a crumbled up paper towel if you want it to look fuller.

Step 5: Assemble The Gnome

To assemble the macrame gnome, use a hot glue gun. Start by applying a generous amount of hot glue to the outside of the wooden ring above the beard, then attach the hat. Next, add more glue to the inside of the beard and secure the nose and mustache beneath the hat. Hold everything in place until the glue cools and sets.

Step 6: Trim The Beard

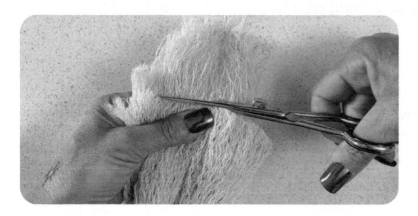

Now it's time to trim the mustache and macrame beard to the desired length. Use the comb and scissors (I like using my hair-cutting scissors) to give it a nice even trim.

Wreath Macrame

Material

- 2-inch brass ring
- Macrame cord (28 strings cut to 22-inch length)
- Thick wool (14 cut 8-inch pieces)
- Comb
- Scissors
- Fabric stiffener (optional)

Step 1: Cut Yarn And Attach It To The Brass Ring

We started the wreath by folding the 22-inch pieces of macrame yarn in half and looping them onto the brass ring with Lark's Head Knots.

This will form a tight circle of yarn that can be sectioned into 7 groups of 8 strings.

Step 2: Knot Diagonal Clove Hitch Knots In V-Shapes Around The Brass Ring

Take the string on the outside of one of the bunch of yarn strings and loop Diagonal Clove Hitch knots toward the center of the group.

Diagonal Clove Hitch Knots are basically loops placed onto the outer string (lead cord) on each side that then meet at the center of the group in a triangular shape.

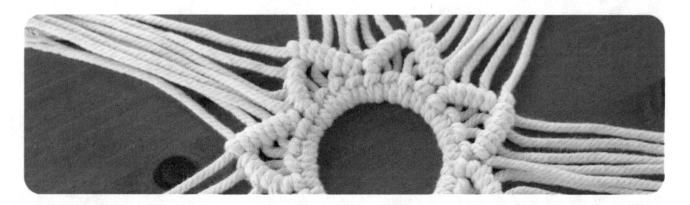

When you go all the way around you will end up with a star shape.

Step 3: Add Another Round Of Diagonal Clove Hitch Knots

Add more Diagonal Clove Hitch knots around the circle over the bottom centers of the last round as shown below. You will end up with short ends which I trimmed and then combed out the edges a little before starting to weave the thick wool yarn into the piece.

52

Step 3: Add Short Strands Of Thick Wool To The Macrame V-Shapes

This step of adding the thick wool is better visible in the video because you have to use the center of the triangular shapes to loop and weave the short pieces of wool through. Similar to a Lark's Head Knot.

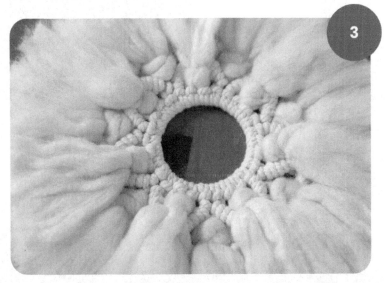

Go all the way around the wreath as shown. You can trim the ends and you are DONE!

Rustic Ornament Macrame

Material

- Willow Sticks
- Hay
- Wood Bead
- Hot Glue
- Scissors

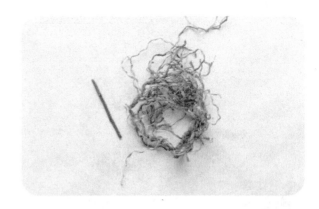

Tutorial Step

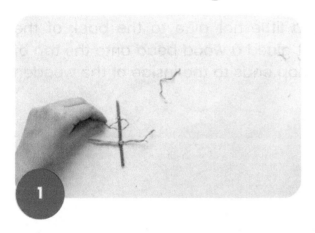

Start with a stick that is the final desired height of the ornament. Then, use lengths of hay to loop together to fill in the green portion of the Christmas tree. Keep these pieces long for ease of tying.

Start with two looped pieces of hay put one under the stick, and the other over, pointing in the opposite direction. Then push the ends of each piece through the loop of the other and pull taut. Repeat this until the tree is full.

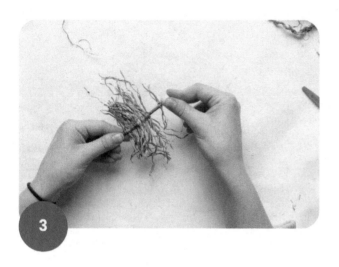

As I added more and more hay I'd apply a little hot glue to the back of the ornament to keep the hay in place. Then I hot glued a wood bead onto the top of the stick. After that, I hot glued the hanging loop ends to the inside of the wooden bead.

Once the stick is filled in with the hay, it is time to trim down the ends of the hay.

I found the easiest way to shape the hay was to start at the bottom and angle the scissors inward toward the top. You will want to create a triangle shape.

Ring Ornament
Macrame

Material

- Macrame core (4mm)
- Wood rings – 2⅝" in diameter
- Wood snowflakes
- Hot glue gun and glue sticks
- Embroidery thread
- Wood beads (12 mm)
- Scissors

Cut the macrame cord to a length of 40 inches. Hot glue one end of the macrame cord to the ring, but leave just a bit of the end overhanging not glued down. This way, you can trim the end back so you will not be able to see it from the front of the ornament. Make sure all the loose threads on the end are secured with hot glue

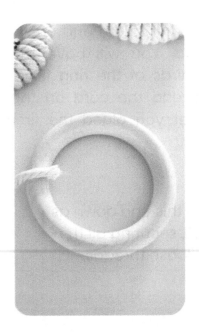
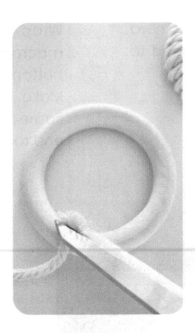

Making The Macrame Ring Cord

1

Start wrapping the macrame cord around the ring. There is no need to glue as you go.

2

Wrap until you get to the end of the macrame cord. You will have the bottom two thirds of the ring filled. Make sure to end the cord on the same side that you glued the first end to initially.

3

Glue this end down as well, securing all the loose threads.

Add The Snowflake To The Ornament

Next, you will be gluing the snowflake onto the macrame cord. Only add hot glue to the bottom two "spokes" of the snowflake. This will allow the snowflake to stand up above the ring. Make sure the snowflake is centered before you press it down. They are a little hard to get off to reposition if you need to, and it ruins the thin wood snowflake if you have to take it off

Add The Embroidery Thread

Next cut a 9 inch piece of cream colored embroidery thread.

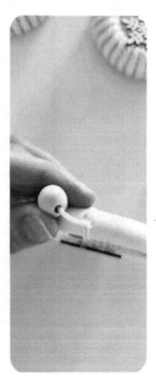

Loop the embroidery thread on the ring and string on a bead. Because the bead will be able to come off of the thread, I hot glued it down to the ring to secure it. Lastly tie a knot at the top of the embroidery thread.

Tree Ornament Macrame

Material

- Macrame cord
- Scissors
- Wood beads (Tree)
- Wood ring (Snowflake)
- White twine (Snowflake)

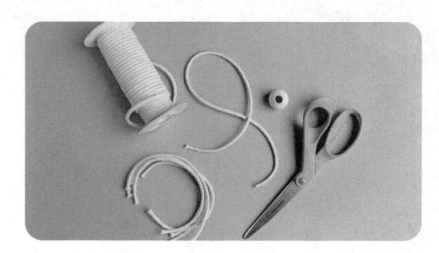

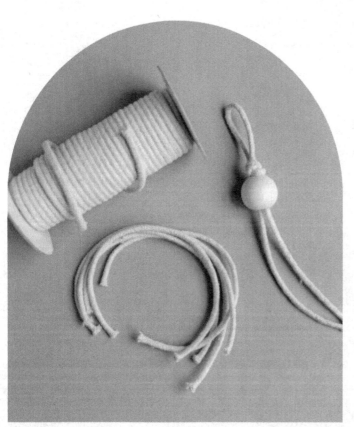

Tutorial Step:

Step 1: Cut 20 pieces of cord eight inches in length, and set aside. Cut one piece of cord about 20 inches in length. Fold the long piece in half and tie a knot below the fold, leaving a two inch loop at the top. String the cord ends through the bead, and pull the bead up to the knot. This will be the center piece of your tree.

Step 2: Start creating your branch pieces by folding one piece of eight inch cord in half and lay it under the center piece with the loop on the left. Fold another piece of cord in half and lay it over the center piece with the loop on the right. Pull the ends of each piece through the loop from the opposite piece and pull tight to create your first knot.

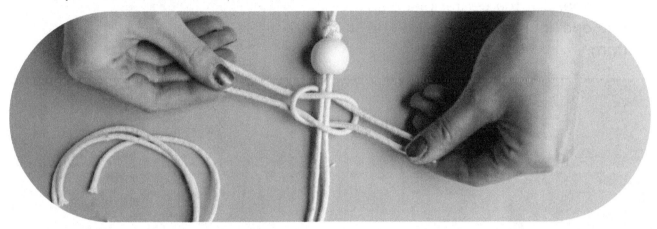

Step 3: Make your second branch by tying the same knot, but this time putting the bottom loop to the right and top loop to the left.

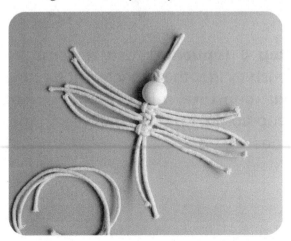

Step 4: Repeat the knots with the remaining pieces of cord, alternating the sides of the loops with each branch.

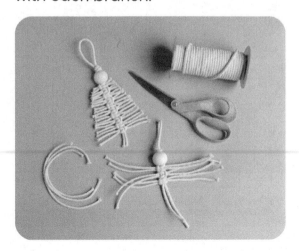

Step 5: Use scissors to cut the branches at an angle to make a tree shape. Cut the center piece so about one inch sticks out on the bottom.

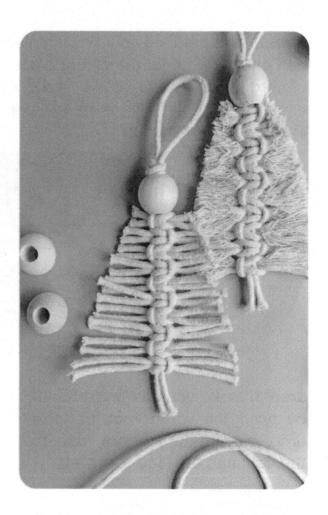

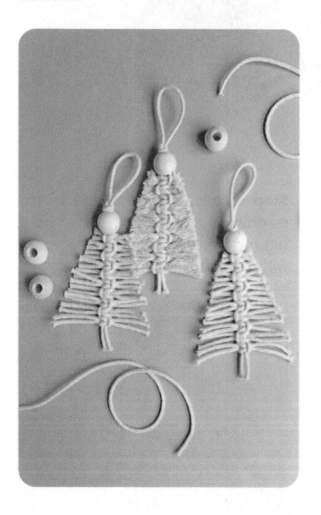

Step 6 (optional): Use a comb or brush to fray the branch pieces (this part can take a little time, but just keep combing). Trim the tree shape, if needed.

Christmas Ornament
Macrame

Material

- Macrame cord
- Scissors
- Wood beads (Tree)
- Wood ring (Snowflake)
- White twine (Snowflake)

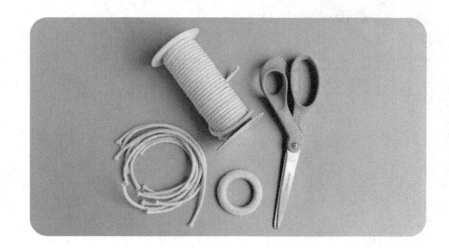

Tutorial Step:

Step 1: Cut 16 pieces of cord eight inches in length. Take one piece of cord and create a larks head knot around the wood ring by folding the piece in half, putting the loop through the center of the ring, and pulling the ends of the cord through the loop.

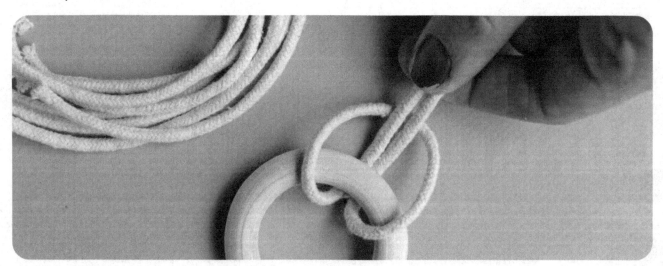

Step 2: Tie larks head knots with the remaining pieces of cord

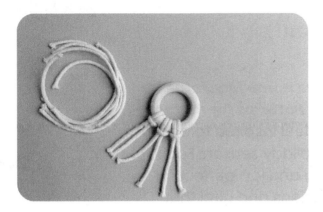

Step 3: Trim the cord pieces to about one and a half inches.

Step 4: Cut a piece of twine to about ten inches. Fold the piece in half and tie a knot half an inch from the top. Attach the twine to the ring with another larks head knot.

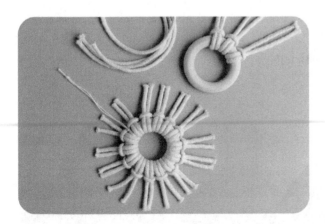

Step 5 (optional): Use a comb or brush to fray the pieces. Trim the snowflake shape, if needed.

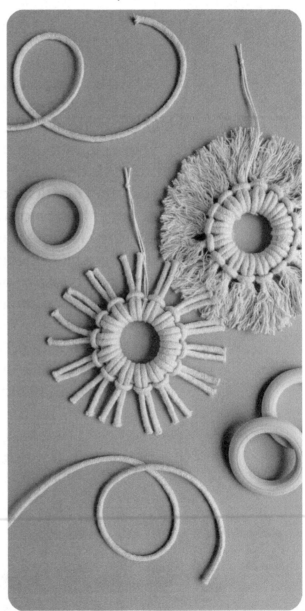

69

Thank you!

As we conclude "*Christmas Home Macramé: Festive Projects and 10 Easy Patterns for Holiday Decorating*," we hope you feel inspired to add your unique touch to the holiday season. Each project is designed for ease and joy, perfect for creating beautiful decorations and gifts that bring warmth to your home.

Macramé is more than knots; it's about the love and creativity woven into each piece. Whether making a festive garland or a handcrafted ornament, these projects let you share your spirit and style.

So, gather your loved ones, experiment, and have fun! Thank you for choosing this book. Wishing you a magical Christmas filled with creativity and joy.

Happy knotting!